SIMPLE RIVER

New and Selected Poems

Sara M. Robinson

Dedication

To Carolyn, as always, my muse

"With water we can always drink, we can cook, we can bathe. And if we are so lucky, we can cleanse."

-J. Burton Hollifield, from *Water Run Down the Mountain*

TABLE OF CONTENTS

The Next-to-Last Canary Speaks

It's a moment.
Our lives are a moment.
It's between those moments
we live,
a space of time
between the blinks
where we crowd in
our tears   laughs   great books
not-so-great poems
and all else that fits.

It's a moment
between solar cyclones,
between trips to the store,
where among the aisles
we pause   hoping to
choose one or two things.

Between the finish line
and the thirteen steps,
before when we
hear something,
a sharp sound

this moment   this vast space
between other moments
where we take a
measure with no markings

creates another space
with no defined depth
or width, but great heights
over which we cannot
see the moments
we forgot to count.

Until this one,
this immeasurable moment,
where time yawns
like a big cat
after swallowing
the next-to-last
canary whose moment
stopped suddenly.

About Soaking Rain

Clouds finally leave
this evening after
pouring their souls
over us for days.

A lone hare
rests in quiet peace
next to an *Arbor vitae*
as the last light falls.

Few storms still brew
over mountains which
swill their froth into mists
carried by stomping tantrums
while I feel the house
shake with last winds.

There is this settledness
at the line between
light and dark as the
hare fades to black.
The trees quiet down,
the birds return to rest.

All is quiet now like
spirits that dine on
whispers of lives
and keep them secret.

A silent, baited trap
is a kind of calm.

Seeded Universe

I pick up these seeds
and rattle them
by my ear:
a deep baritone
          Thock   Thock   Thock.

I turn my head
to catch every syllable
beyond the one dimension.
My inner ear searches
for edges of sound.

The moral truth,
the dark and the light
found in the thock
of a seed
generates lineage
of an earth which contains mine.

A wavy line in an otherwise clear pane.

Universe Slipstream

From the opposite point
of view in space I look
pretty good. I mean
I look young and innocent.

It's amazing what a distance
of four billion miles
can do for your features:
    No black smoke
    No dictatorial crevasses
    No corrupted beaches
            or blighted cities
            or blasted mountaintops
    No polluted rivers
            or dried-up forests

From a distance my heart
and my soul are pure,

like when someone
looks into the jaws
of an open-mouthed
lion and sees that
pretty pink tongue.

The Large is Present in the Small

Sparks fly out the top
of a rusted burn barrel.
Close by a bone-white arm
extends an old broom handle
into the fire and on its end
dangles an unraveling
dirty gray cashmere sweater.

She holds in her other hand
a wad of crumpled wallpaper;
samples found the other day
which served her well
as fine placemats.
Now it's time to burn
them, too.

Her immediate need is heat.
She's cold and the sweater
is too tattered to work
anymore, just threads
of leftover dulled color.

She stands close to
the barrel like she's guarding
a precious sculpture:
    Her burn barrel;
she feeds it and keeps
it lit. She lays claim,

only willing to share
if someone has something
to give; and then they
must hand it to her
so she can place it
on the end of her
burn stick. A ritual
left over from whatever

she had before:
   like the caddy,
   the special pearls,
   enough to eat,
   & her loft in town.

She pushes the sweater
down harder   harder.
Sparks fly up into a void
heat fills up the necessary
space: the one between
her toes and her groin.

Imagine a Flipped Coin

Imagine a stoic Franklin
turning or twisting
in a big circle.

Think of a giant
hand spinning
a big bottle and it points
its neck
        right at yours.

Or a giant hand
flipping a big
coin five miles high.
        (Call it!)

Heads you're infinite,
tails you don't exist.

You try to look
on its underside but
you can't pick it up.
There's this cast
face and it says
nothing to you.

Walking away
you hear
the coin flip.

You race to see
what's on this side.
You miss the chance.
What was underneath
          was meant to stay underneath.

Insomnia

It is torture for me when sleep deprivation sets in or
when it's been robbed from me by outsiders or muggers.

If sleep could be hoarded, hocked, or pawned;
if it could be put under a mattress, saved for a rainy day,
or borrowed from friends or bought on the street
in little glassine bags supplied by baggy-panted sellers
who sold it by the gram, then I would not feel deprived.

It frustrates me when I am so wound up I can't
sleep when I know I must. When I know my muse
is off and on, I realize I am common. I try to write,
but make myself sleepy, counting ripples.
I call me a whirligig when I run all night,
but stay in the same place with thoughts brooding
sulking   dragging deeper   dreading a future.

Dreams pout and whine out dismal, redundant
scenes that bring up the past like sour stomach
or fear of dry heaves soon to a floor nearby. I place
one foot off the bed to stop the spinning, but it doesn't
work, so I apply a cold compress to my head and long
for a pen, now worthless to me, since chucked
out the window. It will hit some unlucky insect

who might actually look up at me, raise a skinny little leg,
point at my tormented demeanor, say in some voice
I can hear and understand: *You know what? You should*

let me bite you. You'll feel better and you can then use
one of my jaws to write out jagged lines that for some

people might even make some sense when they know
it was a mixture of blood and venom that wrote so
well about how you couldn't sleep, and on those nights
when you could, why didn't you hoard it? Save it
for the rough patches, those spots on the mattress
that run together, perpetually hot and sticky.

Purple Barnacles

Knocking purple barnacles
off my poems where
they've been cemented
for ages is too hard
for me to do.

    I don't have the proper tools
    for working underwater.

Any old screwdriver will
do just fine but the best
choice would be the honorable
flat-head: more torque
    best for prying.

You can force those
barnacles loose if you
really want them off.
You have to put your
shoulder elbow wrist
into it. After all
these barnacles stuck
there for a reason,

    and stay on because they can.

I lift my pen to start a line.
I leverage my blade at the edge.
Pressure holds, clamps tight.

This unknown gravity,
this dark force so heavy

becomes a bomb
at the end of a page.

Under the Last Current

How will I feel when
The summer tomatoes at last
are done, when the blossoms
are gone from the squash
and all eggplants are consumed?

No more purples
and yellows at least
on the plants. I'll only
have the fall uniforms
to watch for amidst
grunts and groans
of missed plays, bad calls.

I will miss the warm
nights with moths buzzing
around the porch light.
I will listen better for soft
strings of webs being cast
aloft like exotic sweaters
hanging from tree limbs.

The flowers will start their
hibernation in their clay
pot summer homes.
Down at the pond frogs,
having shooed their summer
offspring off to their own
devices, will start looking

more seriously at shoreline mud,
and think about their best
spots to spend the winter.

But that is still a few weeks
away and now through my
window I wonder if
neighbors will take their
trip as planned after
two false starts today.

While the cool air comes
into my room, I raise
my head to see the squash
are still blooming, giving
a last shout-out probably
with no plans for progeny
among remaining fading leaves,
moving so slowly against
some unknown current.

I Wear These Old Symbols As

Weathered beach glass earrings:
   totems of ancient tribes on a wire.

I feel people
who once held them
in other forms
with dreams of their
own imagined destinies,

or perhaps a wish
for a new day, clearer waters.

I see my friends
we touch
a glass together
or admire some
special snowfall.

I see stones
weathered beneath
clear cold streams–
their purity restated:
   every day is eternity.

When a thousand
years from this
river a wanderer
picks up a satin
shard and turns it over,

will he feel us?

Underground Death-Metal Band Blues

No day is missed where I read about
some malevolent knuckleheads
trying to convince authorities
they are just a little misguided.

They just don't get it, do they?
It's not about them all the time.
It's mostly about what they
leave when they have had
their so-called fun,
when they have left
their so-called message.

And we're supposed to
figure out their intentions,
somehow give them succor,
a pass so they can sneak
back to that hole they
crawled out of, that

place where most of us
would never try to
go, much less find. That
place where those of
us left with any shame would
say we never think about going.

Until some idiot
does something stupid,

like kill people. Then
we find we feel like
we are in that place
where we want to raise
up some arms, do more
than just think, "bang, bang."

Moveable Feast

To speak of boundaries
on a shoreline or view
species whose footprints
are either deep or shallow,
is to see the long-billed
curlew touch down lightly
amidst grasses thick with
their own ecology.

To witness small beetles
and others of similar
exoskeletons going about
their tasks of farming for
mites avoiding the pierce
of one long bill.

But all this is practice
in dwelling among all
who leave such traces
of some existence,
marking balances between
those who feed
those who are fed.

On such justice scales
a slight tip shifts
the whole fulcrum.
Which proves that
there is no perfection

in practice as there is
no perfect boundary
on sand that continuously
moves   will always
shift the footprints.

Creasy Greens

They walk along the banks
on a hot July morning. Mist
on the Shenandoah has
lifted, and in its sleepy
remains are shining, crinkled
leaves of river plants
growing coyly in dense pockets.

These are the wild variety,
not your grocery store hybrids.
They're picked by hardscrabble kids
who live in clapboard homes.
We'll see them later today,

knocking on our door,
buckets held by dirty fingers,
reaching from worn-out sleeves
and faded plaid cotton dresses,
covering skinny muddy legs.
Smiling, sun-burned faces cry

> *All you'd wanna eat–*
> *cook you up a mess of greens–*
> *a quarter a pail.*

The trade of a seasonal
cash crop in their version
of local fair trade is theirs alone.

We're reminded to add sweetened
fatback, as creasies are sharp.

From a coffee can by the stove,
we take out some change,
buy four buckets of scrawny pickings,
and watch as they run
through the briar alley,
pushing shiny coins down
an old holey work sock,
head back to the river

Deep Water Behind the Store

On many Sunday mornings
with my father working
on his store books,
I could hear her wails,
moans, and cries.

Whispers become pleadings,
pouring like cheap whiskey
from most roadhouse nights,
to vaporize out of the jail.

Saturday night's drunken
fun left unpleasant
remnants not especially
kind or considerate given
those circumstances where

a few bruises here and there
from many stumbles
on street curbs were
not mistaken for
any badges of honor.

There were no greetings
or requests for encores;
I was told to ignore
the piercing sounds.

I would hear her laments,
look at my father,
who would frown
go back to his books
on the counter in
front of his prized
miniature whiskey collection.

I found it hard to
read my grammar books
where words fell flat.
I switched attention
to *Endangered Fishes of Virginia.*
I liked the pictures
of the big ones landed

on shore with the men
bone-tired standing around
smiling at their prize catches,
their hands cupping small
glasses of dark liquid.

Obscure Virginia Reels

Lonely holler girl
waits her fate in jail, again,
after another wild
Saturday night,

in a down and out
little gnat of a town
where nothing happens
          good or bad.

Traveling evangelists
set up tents next door
in stale cow pastures
where crowds come round.
Plaid dresses mix with blue jeans
to hear some different news.
          Some good, some bad.

Cars pass by while
shiny pick-ups plow
across broken grass
unload a few to hear
and shake to the good word.

Streets now empty,
dried up in the summer night,
take no notice of
lovers as they "doh-si-doh"
at the regular VFW dance.

Bad words get in the way.
Some drink a little much
Sunday all will be forgiven,
but not for the ones who
crossed over the line.
Not the salvation line, it's
the other one,

the one where you forgot
who you fought and why.
Then you landed your ass
in jail where you listened

to that country holler girl
wail as she did this stupid
two-step to a ratty bunk bed.

Screen Door

Parts of the house
are not fitting right.
The screen door scrapes
on its track and often
pops right out of it.

At that point I get
so mad I yank it
off the frame; then
in my shame I patch
up the holes with
screen band-aids.

It looks like a wounded
warrior who's just about
broken but refuses to give up.
I'm lucky it doesn't break.

After staring at it, I get
out the WD-40, spray
the tracks, and lift
gently as if it were
an invalid who needed

help. It settles back onto
its rails so it can resume
smooth movements,
keep the bugs out,
at least for a while.

I cannot lament
the poor screen's state.
I cannot feel some
tug of guilt at my temper.

I wonder how many
times I can rescue
this impertinent screen; like
I'm some demented nurse
who poisons her charge
then saves as though heroic,
asking why it can't behave.

Why Copperheads Don't Write Poetry

While I put together
a narrative–carefully
spaced words and lines,
do I breathe in poetry
air or loose-lined prose air?

I think I would write
better poetry if I got bit
by an eager Copperhead.

Suppose I found
the snake in our
woodpile hidden under
a blue tarp waiting
for an unlucky field mouse.
I meant to kill it.
I didn't like
that it took in air
that I wanted.

What if the hour-glass
pattern on its skin
held sands not moving
among golds and browns,
that won't fade   but
will take on the black
of death with its foul
air of familiar rot.

Years later I will think
of me with that shovel
telling the snake, I'm sorry,
      (now who has fouled the air)
just before I killed it.

The cool fall air.
The wooden handle.
The metal spade.
The dry skin.
The dirt.

A Sky of Indeterminate Species

Life does not exist on other planets.
Or if it does, we will not find it,
as our telescope is too short-
sighted to see crucial details
in a big ever-expanding universe.

We are not fitted for extra sense
that appreciates advanced humans.
We do our best work when we arm

for battle thus to conquer,
when ends seem pretty
bloody with such few
good results. Better

to think about vodka
over melting ice
in contained crystal glass
whose elements fused
for gazing through closer
lengths, ignoring distance.

Clarity of glass is an irony
in our elementary hands.
We can peer into what
we believe is infinity
using glass on a stand,
or we can squint as we

kiss a precious liquid
whose fire melts imagination.

When we commence
to talk about outer space,
our mind is relaxed enough
to see waters in buried canals,
across a horizontal plank
of highly polished wood.

To appreciate the distance
from here to there.

Fingers in Cool Waters

I trail behind the others
as we walk along
the small quiet creek.
It is beyond sunrise now,
everyone has announced
they are up   ready
to search for food   mates.

I keep my head low,
listening for any new sound
to tell me something, anything
which would relieve me
of the memories of pictures
I saw this morning.

Bodies burned beyond
any redemption of character.
Buildings brought to knees,
as if concrete was brittle bone.
Anguished faces connected
to scorched   blood-battered
arms   faces show more pain

than we should ever
see in our brief lives.
We live on a dangerous,
wonderful planet where
good news means a day
without some treacherous act,

or some violent gun
event where those who
have can easily destroy
those who have not.
(Try to take a knee)

Amidst all the fury
the rivulets run. Steadiness
of natural rhythms placates
soiled beaches and
hands reach tentatively
I lead them to these waters.

Simple River

"All shall be well and all shall be well and
   All manner of thing shall be well." –Julian of Norwich

I

Our endless exploration
of that we cannot have or own
leads us right back to our origin,
to start the cycle all over.

II

We see this river
and we want to run
blindly through it.
Our shouts catch
in splashes like
we are children
when adults half-listen
to our rushed words
and high-pitched exclamations.
Depth soundings   Soundings of now
     Soundings of always
Simple river   so complex

III

They told us.
They told us we would.
They told us we would be.
They told us we would be well.

IV

Their words set us on fire.
We would be hot coals
where none but we could walk.

V

Cooling waters wait
for those who thirst.

Occoquan Path

Blues, greens, browns, blacks, whites.
Colors emerging from soggy grounds.

Wonderful Wetlands

says the sign as we tread pathways
close to dark brown bay waters that

became choked at shore with
plastic bottles, unnatural body parts.

The lap, lap, lapping of the bay
The same no matter what it meets

From manmade machines molded
into facsimiles of natural shapes

which having washed up were bound
in driftwood branches, captured
twisted-shelled snails who
had struggled for their own shores.

The lap, lap, lapping of the bay
The same no matter what it greets

As its chords play out against crowded
shores I can't ignore, my footsteps,
quiet, purposeful, move around objects

as if to avoid disturbance of human remnants,
a comb, a helmet, tires.

What had this bay, this land, looked like
before we all appeared?
An unspoiled vista, seen as pure?

Are we just one more invasive species
with our own transfigurations?
A change in form, a change in locality.

Nevertheless, all this will remain
floating in its own assembly
on earth in the only quantity
it has, and as far as we know
forever with its chorus

> Lap, lap, lapping
> Of the bay that
> Sounds the same.

Martini Supernova

In space if there are
explosive sounds that
shatter any quiet among
drifting planets we
don't hear it in our
everyday lives.

The noise out there is
somehow a music for
others' appreciation
and in its preparation
for some huge
cosmic event we
all will be dazzled.

Inside my martini glass
it is quiet and serene.
The only explosion
I hear is the crunch
of a green caperberry,
a lonely sphere suspended
by no particular law of gravity.

We are all suspended
in the medium of this
immediate part of the universe,
where stars and planets
start and collide everyday.

I feel like a supernova
moving toward earth
where I'll fly by,
since I can't stop,
I'll wave and hope
that somebody sees me.

What if I Caught

poems talking to each other,
or even more tantalizing,
I caught them doing the nasty.

Poems have been heard
giving their love
out all over town.
No control   No one
stopping them 'cause
no one is looking for them.

Note to self: I'm just taking
this on as it's that time
of year and I'm reacting
to the vexing isolation

No battles are being
planned around poems
crossing over forbidden
borders where there
won't be any wars
fought over poems
stealing anyone's water rights.

What if I dreamed
of the end of the world
where the only poems
alive spoke of wars
and gene-twisted crops?

Verses, which retreated,
hid to become artifacts
likely buried   forgotten.

What if I woke up
and found I was
swimming in this
water where words
replaced all the jellyfish
Lionfish   trash   oil spills.
Would I be lucky or what?

The Bridge

I walk on the bridge.
It crosses the Shenandoah
and no cars meet
or pass me as I step
foot by foot
on my slow path.

The pavement, hot against
my feet, offers neither
comfort nor resistance,
as the river flows below,
unaware of my slow
tread above it.

With its own purpose,
a contented course planned
out millions of years ago.
I search for mine with
far less time to find my way.

Soft, bland mountains
face me without challenge
or malice, and though
they are close enough
to touch they offer
no closeness for me.

Their presence, a crowd
in the sky, competes for space

with all that flies within.
I wonder how long
they will last. I hope
I won't outlast them.

I see the town
in my approach
with the first white
buildings hogging the
road between green trees
whose limbs shade yards
and guard residents.

No one can see me.
I am so swift or I am
too slow as gray heads
rise up from tending
flowers and turn toward
an invisible sound.

I stop to wave hello,
but seeing no one
they resume their chores.
I have waited too long
for my return.   I missed
my chance to see ones
I knew, loved, forgot.

None are in their usual
spots: the store, the doctor's,
the post office, the lunch counter.
My memory formed outlines

like a forgotten new coloring
book; and its vacant lines
with no substance wait
for pink or blues or greens.

No life fills up the blanks,
I ask the sky where am I
supposed to be.

Perhaps I am not
in my usual spot either.

Where Did You Hear

that I was not planning
to come back to live
in the little town
by the little river?

Both are too small
for the largeness
that I require.
The space between

water and land
must be wide
enough to hold
the air between

my outstretched arms,
the number of breaths
I must take to fill up

my life. It is my
way   the only
plan I know
where it works.

I dodge all
the small things
in hopes that
I land on the
large ones.

Ones that tell me
I saw the world
and fell back
down to earth.

A Condensed History of Words

When I write of my small-town roots
dug in beside split mortar and broken bricks,
I'm not selling out to a bigger scheme.

I'm not fearful of going further nor
do I abandon my native soil, winsome
prairie that it is.

I feel my localism fed from creasy greens.
My speech is a long-gone clumsy blend
of eastern European and middle Elktonian.

Forged into this amalgam is southern vernacular
education with spring water-induced syntax,
learned from the confluence

of cultures babbling around
our family store. Mountains
holding forth over deep hollows

create originality only locals can grasp,
speak of, cry over. I feel the arable
earth plowed by sunburned fellows

whose farms bordered our town. I see
the soil on their skin; the sun, and rain
in their eyes. They speak of crops,

homes, tool sheds which hold
family treasures, crammed into
faded orchard boxes and dented

biscuit tins. I wish I could see
their places, eat off their cracked-tile
kitchen floors, sit on their squeaky

porches. Then I could really feel
what it must be like to speak
words born from dark, buttery earth.

Hallelujah

Pieces of chicken
in the cast iron skillet
slowly simmer,
send their aromas
through the kitchen
and out to the porch,

where I sit on a bench
watching the river,
listening to kd lang
sing *Hallelujah*,
thinking for the world
how lucky I am how
in love I am with all
that belongs with me.

Maybe it was the scotch,
but I could swear I
heard the voices of all
I have ever known and loved,
then I knew how
much I miss you.

Time becomes seamless for me.
I count every second
hold on to it
for as long as I can.

As I let one go, then catch
another, I see us for
a brief moment–
We are eighteen.

I turn for a closer look,
the river is still moving.

River Stones

By the time it takes
for molecules and
atoms to connect,
flow toward the sea
disperse   dilute,
they will lose any
chance for individuality.

But speak to me
of this running of words.
This running of tides,
rivulets along shores
that move themselves
over time. Never are
we sure where
they will end their quest.

These earthly habits keep
up their work, never
mind me or us. We are
not part of the equation.
We contrived our own
math to explain why
we fixate on pebbles
we throw across water,
in hopes of making
a perfect skip; but they
all sink ultimately, no
matter how perfectly
they are thrown.

Christmas on the Shore

I found the place on the map
when we left for our last trip.
It is the road that went along
the river, the one with all
the turns north and south.

We stayed in that cute little cottage,
the one on the water's edge with
the broken heater, and stove
with one working burner.

We had Christmas there one year
with the last spindly tree which
seemed happy to see us when
we reluctantly gave the clerk
five dollars for it.

We hung all our ornaments
we brought on its skinny arms,
secured it next to the fireplace,
praising how good it looked
all dressed up.

We laughed at the cold, waited
for the sleet to stop, felt our own
heat build inside asking if it was
alright to be consumed.

The fireplace crackled its permission
with one last log placed. We
sprinted for the comforter, nestled
on the sofa, smiled at the tree
closed our eyes.

Funny how some things
just beg to be touched.

Sometimes a Love Tap

It was in the fall
we felt the heat
the beach fried
below our feet,

on our necks
scorched our backs
as we watched fishermen
toss bait nets out
between the sand bars.

Live bait ran ahead
of large-toothed fish
prowling shallows
for expected feasts.

One young man
fought for an hour
to land a bull shark
just ahead of us,
where we swam

the day before.
As we looked,
questioning each other,
I wondered if the soft
nick I felt earlier

on my heel now bleeding
back at the cottage,
was a love tap
from an undesired suitor.

Something underneath that water
confusing me for bait,
giving me a little taste
of what nibbling is like.

Toward an Evening Sunset

As I look west
out my window
I gaze at fading trees,
exhausted shrubs,
waiting for the last
of the day.
They are limp
from all the glad greetings
greetings they give
as part of their daily routines.

They want to rest now,
be idle for a while.
No more working hard,
they want only to breathe.

I know how they feel.

Sometimes all I want
to do is breathe,
not think of anything
else but how it feels
just to take in a breath,
let it out, not worry
about saying a word.

Think how wonderful
that sunset is. If I
said anything, if I dared

to spoil the tenderness,
it would ruin all the colors.

How Fine the Line

When I can see the edge
of the river and the sun
has just about closed
her rim, I know
the next sight will
be the brilliance
of her special green
flash. After that I
can stroll back
to our cottage,
wait for the next
day with more
enthusiasm than
I arrived with.

I'll be able to see
how the trees
outline the road.
Road outlines
the plain. Plain
outlines the state.
State outlines
the country. Country
outlines the continent.
Continent outlines
the oceans and oceans
hold all the lines.
Always will. So
this line of saltwater

in my plastic cup
is only one little
measure of a
much larger truth.
That truth of
knowing when
I ask you if
you feel the same
way you have
always felt
about me, you
say I might have
crossed the line.

Bedrock

I am stones under the river
worn smooth by washing
souls, lost fishing lures,
parts of broken cities, ramparts
from bridges and a few old cars.

Fish have grazed on my skin
crawfish have darted under me.
I have sheltered eggs, gelled larvae,

and broken bones. I am monolithic,
metamorphic with great patience
under extreme pressure. You

can throw me across streams.
I'll pretend to skip, make you
smile, but I won't come back.
You can walk on me but in a wink
I can wreck your canoe.

I've tumbled down paths many will
never travel. My core is solid.
I have memories trapped. I can
be cracked open, shoveled around.
The smaller I get the more my resolve sticks.

Under this river, time flows over me.
I am the hourglass re-set for eons.
I am the bottom, the bedrock,
the unpredictable one.

My Life Has Unfolded and Been Re-mapped Like Origami Paper Put Into Motion By a Few Crucial Creases

I thought by now I
would have figured it all
out. Pulled my future

out of a clamshell, no
fortune cookie for me,
since I realized I

came from beside
the river. I grew up
along this fast-moving

body which I thought
like me wanted to get
the heck out of town.

But the river, it stayed.
I was the one who
left and like most

who find they seek
other streams, other
liquids for life,

I found eddies, twisty
currents for the most
part. My job

was to forge them
into channels which

would lead me
to broader,
wider currents,

which I could
then take around
the world or at least

from north to south
or at least from
one small town

to a slightly
larger one, where
I could fix

my own coordinates,
divine my own
future with my

own carved rod,
which when held
in just the right

way could find
waters of the best
sweetest kind:

waters that could
save me from
thinking always

of my past,
worrying too much
about how to change

it, when all I needed
was to look at where
I was going.

The river taught
me all that and
it didn't even

know it was
working hard
for my liberation,

my ability to
navigate around
trash and chaos,

around worldly pathos
for which I was
helpless. Even

if I were helpless,
what could I possibly
have done to have

any effect on others.
Here I am now: I am
a poet, I say you can't

trust a poet to
give you exercise
advice. No poet

can tell you how
to bench press
your own weight,

or what weight
barbell to lift
over your head.

You can't rely on
a poet to give you
wellness information

about what you
should do after
the holidays

to shed those
acquired pounds
invasive inches,
which now

reside precisely
where you swore
you would never

gain an inch.
        Ah, but I digress.

The river is what
I am discussing here,
this flowing course
of information never

ceasing its babbling
of tell-all and see-all.
Yet we will stop

what we are doing
whenever anyone says
we should go down

look at the river.
What will we see? It
moves. It always moves.

It will always
move on while we
will someday stop

take no more steps
toward any place,
Going nowhere, but

over time, everywhere;
unless we are trapped
in some arbitrary vessel

where we will remain
bound   caged
not able to free

our atoms or let
nature take us
on further journeys,

where some small
part of what remains
of us might actually

have a chance
to make a difference.

Still I digress. We do

have our portions
in life to choose
from if we so

desire. We do have
options to choose,
paths to contemplate.

Think about that
last piece of coconut
cake that you ate

over the holidays.
It was your second
one waiting there

just for your love.
You didn't think
about your past.

You thought for
a second about
the next week

decided like
the river decides.
It's all about

heading in the right
direction, it's all
about portion control.

The River Was the Only Thing Going

From behind the wheelhouse a slight
trickle of water entered the already
swollen stream. Neither the mill

nor the stream felt any lasting
impressions of their journeys.
Stones and water converged

in ways man has mastered
or at least accepted. With his
intrusion came the unexpected,

the mess when his devices failed.
Derailments spilling contaminations
added fuels which don't bring

promises of new energy. Dirtiness
of spoils pitted the refugees
of life against each other.

When we drank or when
we breathed, we gasped
in our struggles in our life's

river with its corrugated water,
abundant turbulence, its churning
frothing destiny.

Titration

Take me slowly, a drip
at a time for I want
to feel like I have
been used in the
best recipes, cooked
in the darkest broths,
baked in the
warmest suns.

The Town Speaks by the River

The dwelling starts with those
within and those without. We
take hold of timbers attach
braces with sturdy hands
and willing backs. Our stories
will emerge to unfold in lines,
phrases, peppered grateful
pauses. We are the underpinning
of this town where our breaths
hold the precious air between us
and our mountains.

When you see each of us alive
in our moments, will you see our
hands clasped together or
will our hands hold our young
or those of others?
In our suits we take in how
serious our lives are in life,
in death. We go nowhere
but we are everywhere. We speak
in new ways. In our voices
you will hear our poetry.

The words are simple, really. They
reveal us in our capture, the
one that binds us with shackles
of wheat straw and offers up
river water of clearest taste and
hints of freedom in its rapids.

The Long Southern Good-bye Talks and Swoons Over

Histories That Cover Ages of Us: Them   We   You   Continues
Its Soliloquy Over Food   Porches   Bicycles   Gardens   Hollows
Pools   Rivers   Beaches   Coconut Cake   Brothers   Mothers
Cousins   Weddings   Spouses   Others   All the Significant Details
Spread Out   Like a Big Banquet   Where We Consume   Bits
and Pieces of
Well-done Lives   Slightly Rare Personas   Where We Absorb All
Whom We Knew   or   Thought We Did   Who We Readily
Gave Up
So We Wouldn't Have to Know Them Better   and in That Moment

we walked through this screen door,
the one that can't stay on track.
While we faked a sincere grin,
our eyes sighted something
on a distant horizon—
A silvery, shimmering thread:
a pounding current, speaking.

Acknowledgements

Hallelujah and *The Bridge* previously appeared in or were modified from <u>Two Little Girls in a Wading Pool</u> (2012, Cedar Creek Publishing)

I Wear These Old Symbols previously appeared in <u>A Cruise in Rare Waters</u> (2013, Cedar Creek Publishing)

Deep Water Behind the Store and *Obscure Virginia Reels* previously appeared in <u>Stones for Words</u> (2014,Cedar Creek Publishing)

www.ingramcontent.com/pod-product-compliance
Lightning Source LLC
LaVergne TN
LVHW091124180726
843490LV00002B/940